Faith, Hope, and a Sense of Humor

FAITH, HOPE, AND A SENSE OF HUMOR

HOW TO SURVIVE AND THRIVE ON THE FRONT LINES OF PARISH LIFE

KAREN L. BAKER

Our Sunday Visitor
Huntington, Indiana

Copyright © 2022 by Karen L. Baker

27 26 25 24 23 22   1 2 3 4 5 6 7 8 9

Our Sunday Visitor Publishing Division

Our Sunday Visitor, Inc.
200 Noll Plaza
Huntington, IN 46750
www.osv.com
1-800-348-2440

ISBN: 978-1-68192-690-2 (Inventory No. T2564)
1. RELIGION—Christian Ministry—Pastoral Resources.
2. RELIGION—Christianity—Catholic.
3. RELIGION—Christian Living—Spiritual Growth.

eISBN: 978-1-68192-691-9

LCCN: 2022938918

Cover design: Tyler Ottinger

Cover art: Adobe Stock

Interior design: Chelsea Alt

PRINTED IN THE UNITED STATES OF AMERICA

For my late father, Meinrad Lang, who always showed what God's mercy looks like. And for my mother, Jane, a living witness to faith, hope, and love after ninety-two years on earth.

CONTENTS

INTRODUCTION

I like to define virtue as a holy habit, but if you want to hear a more official explanation, the *Catechism of the Catholic Church* defines virtue as "an habitual and firm disposition to do the good" (1803). The goal of a virtuous life, the paragraph continues, is to "become like God." That is quite a goal! How are we to reach that goal? What and who can help us get there?

In pondering this larger-than-life invitation to become like God, especially in parish ministry, a thought occurred to me: As important as our office supply closet is — fully stocked with paper, pens, clips, and things that have been left in there since the place was built — there is an even more crucial "closet" in every Catholic parish, a closet stocked with virtue. It's not hard to find; in fact, it is the focal point of every church. It is the Tabernacle, where the living God resides. We need to visit this closet often, avail ourselves of the Lord's presence, and make sure we follow Saint Paul's advice: "Put on then, as God's chosen ones, holy and beloved, heartfelt compassion, kindness, humility, gentleness, and patience" (Col 3:12).

After working in my home parish for almost twenty years — twelve as a volunteer and seven as a full-time employee — I've realized that faith, hope, and a sense of humor are crucial to parish ministry, whether you are on staff or offer your time and talent as a volunteer. In fact, all of the virtues (more later on how a sense of humor can be a virtue) are necessary to survive and thrive amid the sometimes-chaotic world of parish life. Growing in virtue, however, is a challenge, despite the mistaken assumption that working in a Catholic context would automatically provide a prime place for becoming a better Christian.

This book has been germinating/percolating/steeping in my head and in my heart for several years, and it came about for a few reasons. First, there has been tremendous growth in the number of lay ministers in the Catholic Church over the past sixty years, since Vatican II. "As of 2013, the estimated number of lay ecclesial ministers in the United States was approximately 38,000 (2.1 per parish). 14% of these are vowed religious and 86% are other lay persons."*

That number increases each year, and yet it seems that resources to support those involved in parish ministry are in short supply. Parish staff members work long hours for little pay, volunteers work countless hours for no pay, and although none of us are in this for the glory or the money, we could all use a little

---

* Office of Public Affairs, "Laity and Parishes," United States Conference of Catholic Bishops, https://www.usccb.org/offices/public-affairs/laity-and-parishes.

encouragement. I hope this book provides some.

The second thing that prompted me to write this book came from my formation in theological and pastoral studies. There, I learned that growing in virtue is both a right and an obligation: "As he who called you is holy, be holy yourselves in every aspect of your conduct, for it is written, 'Be holy because I [am] holy'" (1 Pt 1:15–16). That's a challenge! I pray this book helps you tackle it.

Finally, as someone who struggles to grow in every virtue, I thought a reflection on parish ministry in light of the virtues might help everyone in the vineyard of the Lord, including me. That is: I needed to write this book in order to practice what I preach!

I invite you to join me as I reflect on ministry during both "ordinary" and extraordinary times. All of it is, I hope, a resource to help us grow in holiness to serve the people of God who make up a parish, whether in their homes, at work, or in our pews.

May we all open ourselves to God's grace so that we can grow in the virtues needed to survive, thrive, and serve his people well.

1

FORMED IN FAITH, SENT TO SERVE THROUGH EMAIL

FAITH

"We walk by faith, not by sight."
— 2 Corinthians 5:7

Life has been interesting so far, I'll say that. I worked in the newspaper business for thirty years, writing headlines, editing stories, and coordinating community news with a helpful little column that served my corner of the world by alerting residents to food drives, school news, art festivals, local theater, and much more. Some mocked my work as "Cub Scout News," but so be it! It fit me well.

Somewhere along the line, when my pastor at the time wanted to make sure parish and school pictures were printed in the local paper, he found out about my newspaper connection and invited me to help make that happen.

The little door that opened and led me to encounter God in a most powerful way. I saw all these wonderful, faith-filled people committed to caring for the poor, visiting the sick, and handing on the Faith. Meanwhile, I was stuck in the mud. I was a poorly catechized cradle Catholic married to a non-Catholic who had lots of questions I realized I couldn't answer. Also, I had personal worries, problems, and concerns. Too fearful to talk to a priest, I worked up the courage to bring these worries and problems to a deacon, who led me to RCIA and encouraged me to learn more about the Faith so I would have the tools to live it and share it more fully. The rest is history — sort of.

That is, once I went through the RCIA process, I fell in love with the beauty of our Faith, with the God who loves us so abundantly. I ended up on the Pastoral Council, started taking classes at the Loyola Institute for Ministry, and then, just after graduating from Loyola, something big happened: The newspaper where I worked laid off two hundred people, including me.

I was on a pilgrimage to the Holy Land when I got the call about losing my job. There I was, walking on the shore where Jesus walked, with a newly minted master's degree in pastoral studies and no job. What could Jesus be calling me to do? First, I decided to apply for a new lay formation program through Notre Dame Seminary in the Archdiocese of New Orleans. I had no job, so why not? I love learning, and I had time on my hands.

I also needed a paycheck to support my family, however, and so I found creative ways to make a living: I cobbled together some part-time work here (in my parish) and more part-time work there (at a Catholic school), with assorted freelance writing assignments in between. Eventually, I started a full-time position as administrative assistant for the superintendent of Catholic schools. But in 2015, the new pastor of our parish decided he would like to hire an office manager. I am eternally grateful that he hired me.

Though I have had my ups and downs filling the role, I felt God had called me to this place, to serve in the parish that I love. My years of study were being put to great use! Then one day, not long after I started the office manager gig, someone walked into my office and asked me: "Do you feel you've wasted your formation?"

In other words, "Why are you a secretary when you've got a master's degree in pastoral ministry and were commissioned by the archbishop (through the aforementioned lay ecclesial ministry program)?" I explained to her what I would love to explain to anyone who doesn't understand the workings of a parish office: There is plenty of ministry being done behind a desk, and a great deal of ministry done by the person who takes Mass intentions and answers the phone (you know, as the face and voice of the parish!). Ministry occurs when "two people toast their glasses of wine and something splashes over," as Henri Nouwen so beautifully put it in *Jesus: A Gospel*. He continues: "Ministry is the overflow of your love for God and for your fellow human beings."

So don't let anyone tell you that a receptionist or office manager or bookkeeper or volunteer greeter or usher or church cleaner is not doing ministry when working in a Catholic (or any other denomination) parish. And don't forget: If you fill any of those roles, you are most certainly engaging in ministry.

Why? Well let's go a bit further in defining that slippery little word.

Ministry is official service to the church, service to God's people, to build up his kingdom. As Thomas O'Meara defines it in *Theology of Ministry*, it is "the public activity of a baptized follower of Jesus Christ flowing from the Spirit's charism and an individual personality on behalf of a Christian community to proclaim, serve and realize the kingdom of God."

So, yes — every email is ministry; the Facebook posts, phone calls, rearrangement of the parish calendar, those are ministry too. And the widow who comes to your desk to schedule Masses for her husband but really just wants you to listen so she can tell you how much she misses him — that is most certainly ministry. It is ministry because it is all official business on behalf of the community to proclaim, serve, and realize the kingdom. And if the kingdom is God's love breaking through in this messy world (and it is!), all of your little mundane tasks are kingdom builders. The emails you craft with kindness, the calls you answer with love, the comments you get after Mass about the flower arrangement being too big or too little or not the right color — the way you respond to those comments, when you dig down deep to find kindness — well, that's ministry, because you just showed someone what heaven looks like.

When someone walks in looking for a priest but finds only you, then you are called to be the face of Christ. In fact, we are all called to be the face of Christ in each and every encounter, whether we are on staff or serving as volunteer ushers, greeters, readers, etc. When someone treats you like a servant, remember that you are. So is he or she. We all are. We serve the people of God, and we are the people of God. When someone asks if you've wasted formation by being formed for ministry when you're "just a secretary," remember that there are no "justs" in the business of bringing forth the kingdom of God. (Also remember that secretaries are often the glue that keep a place together!)

The kingdom is for the lost, lonely, outcast, the office workers, maintenance supervisors, and volunteers as well as for deacons, priests, and bishops. The kingdom of God also exists beyond the boundaries of office and church.

We are called to serve everywhere we go in this upside-down world that Jesus shows us in the Gospels. On some days, we may not see how what we do has any impact at all. We may get stuck in the details of a spreadsheet or caught up in a drama between one person and another; we may even end up spending hours moving boxes of books out of one closet to make room for more boxes and then try to figure out where to put the boxes we just took out. (This happens all the time! Parish ministry is full of moving things.) I may wonder, "Where is God in all of that? Did I need a degree to organize closets?" Maybe.

It's all a matter of faith. We may not see the fruits of our labors, but we have faith that what we do, when done with love, builds up God's kingdom. Also, it's not at all about what we do anyway; instead, it's about who we are. Are we grumpy while answering the phone or unloading boxes or tabulating RSVPs for the volunteer social? Or are we joyful? If we have faith in God's grand plan, we will serve with a joyful heart. But yes, sometimes it is hard.

That's why we need to get back to the supply closet full of virtue and fill up on faith.

ॐ

Virtue: Faith
As Lived and Taught by Jesus: Matthew 14:25–31
How does Jesus show us the importance of faith and trust in God? For me, what comes to mind is Peter when he encounters Jesus walking on the water:

> During the fourth watch of the night, he came toward them, walking on the sea. When the disciples saw him walking on

the sea they were terrified. "It is a ghost," they said, and they cried out in fear. At once [Jesus] spoke to them, "Take courage, it is I; do not be afraid." Peter said to him in reply, "Lord, if it is you, command me to come to you on the water." He said, "Come." Peter got out of the boat and began to walk on the water toward Jesus. But when he saw how [strong] the wind was he became frightened; and, beginning to sink, he cried out, "Lord, save me!" Immediately Jesus stretched out his hand and caught him, and said to him, "O you of little faith, why did you doubt?"

Taking our eyes off Jesus can lead us to flounder. Keeping our focus and faith, that's what keeps us moving.

ભ

TO PONDER

Do I have faith that I am where God calls me to be?

How do I know when it's time to make a change in ministry?

What do I do when I question my place in ministry?

What can I do to cultivate the virtue of faith each day?

2

ENCOUNTERING JESUS TOGETHER, EVEN WHEN WE ARE APART

HUMILITY

"Walk humbly with your God."
— Micah 6:8

"The first pastoral commandment is closeness: being close to the people."[*] Pope Francis uttered those words in Rome in 2015. Closeness. A beautiful thought. A pastoral necessity. And, from 2020 through early 2022, a tremendous challenge.

This book began before the world came to a screeching halt

---

[*] Joshua J. McElwee, "Francis: First Commandment of Parish Life is Closeness to People," *National Catholic Reporter,* March 10, 2015, https://www.ncronline.org/blogs/francis-chronicles/francis-first-commandment-parish-life-closeness-people.

in March 2020; that is, it began before the COVID pandemic pressed a giant pause button on life as we knew it. Suddenly, it seemed, the "closeness" Pope Francis encouraged just a few years ago became a distant memory, even a potential danger to our health and wellbeing.

But what about spiritual health? What's a parish to do for the People of God when public Masses are suspended or limited? How do we serve others when community life vanishes and then struggles to come alive? Ministering in a parish in that context seems impossible. It seems paradoxical, in fact. Does a parish even exist if there are no people in the pews?

Well, of course it does. In fact, one of the many lessons the pandemic taught me — taught all of us — was this: The "parish" exists outside of this collection of buildings on our campus. It exists in the homes and hearts of those who profess the Catholic Faith and live it out in their kitchens, schools, and workplaces.

The parish is the Church alive and breathing in the world. This is how St. John Paul II described it in his document *Christifidelis Laici* (On the Vocation and Mission of the Lay Faithful):

> The ecclesial community, while always having a universal dimension, finds its most immediate and visible expression in the parish. It is there that the Church is seen locally. In a certain sense it is the Church living in the midst of the homes of her sons and daughters. (26)

That quote reminds me of something I read from Bill Huebsch in his book *Dreams and Visions: Pastoral Planning for Lifelong Faith Formation*:

> Parish facilities are not the only place where members of the parish meet — the main place they meet is within their homes. So the task of the parish is to provide households with the resources they need to make those household meetings more holy and more intentional. ... The goal is to animate the world with the Spirit of Christ. And the church does that mainly by helping grow and develop households of faith.

So how could we help promote households of faith in the midst of the pandemic — or at any time? What did we learn in the crucible of a health crisis? More than we thought we would. We learned by listening to the prophet Micah: "You have been told, O mortal, what is good, and what the Lord requires of you: Only to do justice and to love goodness and to walk humbly with your God" (6:8).

Amid the masks, hand sanitizer, electrostatic sprayers, floor stickers, and painter's tape, we learned that the only way to face each day was to embrace Micah's trinity of virtues.

Clergy, staff, and parishioners certainly did practice goodness and mercy, arranging for drive-up confessions and checking on the lonely and elderly. We also did our best to act justly, following rules and looking out for our most vulnerable brothers and sisters. Most importantly, though, in the chaos of pandemic life, it was walking humbly, the virtue of humility, that helped us survive and thrive day to day. In many ways, the Church that walks humbly came alive during the pandemic.

How so? It may be helpful to think of walking humbly with God this way: It's like when a small child walks humbly with a parent or grandparent, taking his or her hand, listening with love and following along. During the 2020 shutdown, my parish's clergy, staff, and parishioners took God's hand and let him lead the way. In doing so, we learned many things that continue to serve us well.

We learned about live-streams and the power of video. With God's grace and some good luck, we had installed a live-stream system in our church the year before the pandemic. When the shutdown hit, we put the system to good use. With creativity, our parochial vicar at the time made an array of videos — both fun and informative. His biggest hit was a video to teach people how to have "Mass at home" and provide them with resources to feel as much a part of the Mass as possible. In response, people sent in pictures of their "Mass at home" set-ups. Their living rooms became sacred spaces, and we shared those spaces on social media to remind us that we are, indeed, connected as the Body of Christ. Although we are gratefully gathered again in church, our live-streams still connect with homebound and sick parishioners, and our staff and volunteers continue to harness the power of video in creative ways.

We also learned there was a hunger in parish households, and our clergy responded by going to great lengths to feed the needs of the people. We live-streamed Mass every day; during the shutdown, we also live-streamed the Divine Mercy Chaplet each day and provided a Rosary video each evening. In addition, we live-streamed an all-day May crowning, with parishioners stopping by to bring flowers to our statue of Mary, Queen of Peace and sit in their cars praying the Rosary. It was a beautiful day that brought people together, even when circumstances forced them to stay apart.

We learned about the simple power of a phone call, just to check in and say hello, to offer a prayer and perhaps a trip to the grocery store. A group of staff members and volunteers spent much time on the phone, connecting and offering a ray of hope to those who needed it most. In the absence of Jesus in the Eucharist, our callers brought the presence of Christ to others in the ways that remained possible.

We learned to Zoom, or Google Chat, or FaceTime — whatever we could do to interact, to reach out, to stay connected.

We learned that an email a day from the parish isn't such a bad thing, not when we are trying to be community without physical presence. In that virtual connection we found communion. In that connection, we encountered Jesus together, even when we were apart.

We learned there is great faith in people's homes, where the parish lives and breathes. We don't always see it, but the People of God are sanctifying the world as they are called to do in Vatican II's Dogmatic Constitution on the Church, *Lumen Gentium*: "Led by the spirit of the Gospel they may work for the sanctification of the world from within as a leaven. In this way they may make Christ known to others, especially by the testimony of a life resplendent in faith, hope and charity" (31).

Parishioners gave great testimonies of faith, hope, and charity. For instance, on Good Friday 2020, several families spearheaded a neighborhood Stations of the Cross. Another parishioner coordinated two food drives to feed the hungry. And one week, a group of women decided to borrow an idea they saw on social media, collecting pictures of parishioners and placing them in the pews so our priests would not feel so disconnected or lonely.

We learned that the pandemic called on us to drink from a deep well of virtue. It was, in fact, a strict teacher in the school of virtue, if we were willing to learn, for God speaks through all things.

Many in my parish, many in the Church, humbly listened to God and came up with creative ways to share the Good News in dark times. But this book isn't just about ministry during the pandemic, which I hope is just a memory as you read this. The point is, the humility we practiced during that time opened new doors that can lead to a bright future, as long as we continue our humble journey.

In late 2020, Catholic Leadership Institute CEO Dan Cellucci reminded parishes to look at ministry after the pandemic as a chance to make bold changes. Although churches and parishes wrestled with smaller crowds and collections, and their staffs wondered when or if people would return to the pews, Cellucci advised against asking:

"What if they don't come back?" Instead, he said, we should be asking: "What story will we write?" This new story is full of possibility.

The time of the pandemic invited us to be humble enough to re-imagine parish life, to ask different questions such as: How do we support our households of faith? How do we continue listening for the voice of God, loving, and serving one another as Jesus taught? Are there new ways of sharing the Good News?

We are all called to ask new questions as we stock up on virtue for life and ministry in a parish — the place where the Church, the Spirit of Christ, lives and breathes, the place where we are called to "closeness," physical and otherwise.

☙

Virtue: Humility
As Lived and Taught by Jesus: John 13:12–15
There is no doubt that Jesus gives us a model of humility to follow in ministry. In the Gospel of John, Jesus gives us a powerful example of humility and leadership when he washed the disciples' feet:

> When he had washed their feet [and] put his garments back on and reclined at table again, he said to them, "Do you realize what I have done for you? You call me 'teacher' and 'master,' and rightly so, for indeed I am. If I, therefore, the master and teacher, have washed your feet, you ought to

wash one another's feet. I have given you a model to follow, so that as I have done for you, you should also do."

We are here to serve others. We are here to walk humbly and attentively in the presence of God, following the way of Christ.

ॐ

TO PONDER

What does this Scripture passage say to me about how I serve in the Church?

How does humility help me when facing a crisis?

How do I listen humbly for God amid difficulty?

How could I follow the model of Jesus more closely?

3

HEAR, O ISRAEL!
THE TOILETS ARE BACKING UP

LOVE

"Love never fails."

— 1 Corinthians 13:8

When I go to Mass every Sunday, more often than not there's some little thing I need to take care of, check on, or adjust — usually because of my own forgetfulness (Oops, I didn't put coffee and donuts in the announcements. I'd better fix that!).

There is the occasional Sunday, though, that allows me the chance to celebrate the Lord's Day without distraction. One of these happened on a rainy October Sunday a few years back. It seemed

29

that all I had to do was show up and worship the Lord. No books to put out, no guest speakers to check on, no announcements to update. All was calm, all was cloudy. But then, just seconds into a reading from the Book of Deuteronomy — just as I heard the lector proclaim, "Hear, O Israel!" (or, as the Jewish people say, *"Shema, Yisrael"*) — I felt a tap on my shoulder and heard a whisper in my ear: "Karen, the toilets are backing up!"

I quietly got up while "the Lord is our God, the Lord alone!" echoed in my ears and proceeded to the back of church, checking in with an usher on the toilet trouble. He was working diligently, plunging, and trying to contain the mess, but the problem seemed to grow worse by the minute. Finally, we (well, he, the saintly usher) got it under control. Then I called a plumber to take care of things properly.

Meanwhile, we had soggy, stinky carpet in a couple of places and boxes that needed to be moved: the whole nine yards. But we got it done.

The toilet trouble is just one example of worship and work intersecting, offering parish workers (and volunteers, such as our usher) the challenge of encountering the living God while dealing with very earthy issues.

Although I was happy to help stem the toilet tide that day and am usually happy to do whatever needs to be done on any given day, the truth is this: In parish life, we sometimes long for balance and boundaries, for finding the right mix between work and worship. If you are the office manager, the receptionist, the music director, the director of religious education, or fill any other role in a parish, chances are your Sunday experience will be different from that of the regular church-goer. How can you immerse yourself in the Mass, the "foretaste of that heavenly liturgy" (*Sacrosanctum Concilium*, 8), when you have to make sure everything on earth is in place? It's not easy. What happens when you, dear bulletin editor, walk into church for Mass, longing for the peace you know Jesus will bring, when someone grabs you and says: "Did you know there's a mistake in the bulletin?!" Does it just ruin your day, or can you offer it all up to the Lord?

These are the challenges we face in parish ministry. There is no escaping your role when you walk into Mass at the church where you serve. However, there are ways to preserve your well-being, and still serve God's people.

Occasionally, when I truly need some peace, I visit a neighboring parish for Mass or even for a quiet morning prayer. I also have found that if I attend one of our less crowded Masses, I can slip in the side door, worship the Lord, and slip out without too much trouble. Finally, I have learned that it is OK and sometimes necessary to say "No, I'm dashing off to take the kids to lunch" or "Can you call me Monday?" when requests are made before, during, or after Sunday Mass. When we speak the truth with charity, people almost always understand.

So yes, there are some ways to set your work/worship boundaries, even if it means occasionally worshiping elsewhere. But what I have discovered is this: Though the liturgy next door (three miles away) is beautiful, though the Lord is still present, something is missing! And I know what it is. It's my community, my brothers and sisters whom I love and serve every day. The Church is made present in many ways — in the sacramental life, especially. But I find God powerfully manifested in the community of believers who make up my parish. When I kneel after Communion and watch people returning to their pews, I see faces full of love, sorrow, and joy. I wonder what they each carry in their hearts, and I pray they feel the comfort of the Sacrament that has opened a great big door to grace. As I kneel there, I also notice the marks on the wooden pews where my folded hands rest. I think about all the rosaries and rattles and keys that may have made their marks on this wood. I think about all the emotions that are brought into this space for weddings, baptisms, and funerals. And I think of the many hands that have been folded on this pew, of all the prayers people have laid at the feet of Jesus.

At times like these, I know without a doubt that it is a blessing to work where I worship. I also know that I need to make regular trips to the supply closet full of virtue to see what will help me along this journey. I need to grow in virtue so that I can not only survive, but also thrive.

The virtue I know I need to deal with the work/worship issue is this: Love. I love the God who loves me. I love the people of God who make up this family of faith where I minister. No matter the tap on the shoulder, the flowing of the toilets, the emergency alerts to typos

in the bulletin, I am called to love as God commanded us to love —
the way he loves us. I am called not just to recite the Jewish *Shema*,
"Hear, O Israel, the Lord is our God, the Lord alone!" but to love my
neighbor as myself. My neighbors are sitting next to me in the pew,
and I am to love them. They may be sitting at home, perhaps in need
of a call or a visit, and I am to love them there. I love God for who he
is and for calling me to serve him. I love Jesus for showing me what
God's love in action really means — sacrifice and service.

And so, I worship where I work, just as you might do. The days
can be challenging enough, and there are definitely times in which we
have to say "no," even times when we need to go elsewhere for Mass
to find peace. But while it may sound trite, home really is where the
heart is. If you love your parish family, you can endure all of the questions, complaints, and bad plumbing that come your way, with the
assurance of Saint Paul's words to the Corinthians:

> Love is patient, love is kind. It is not jealous, is not
> pompous, it is not inflated, it is not rude, it does not seek
> its own interests, it is not quick-tempered, it does not
> brood over injury, it does not rejoice over wrongdoing
> but rejoices with the truth. It bears all things, believes all
> things, hopes all things, endures all things. Love never
> fails. (1 Corinthians 13:4-8)

☙

Virtue: Love
As Lived and Taught by Jesus: John 13:34–35

Saint John tells us that "God is love" (1 Jn 4:8). Just before his death, Jesus tells his Apostles: "I give you a new commandment: love one another. As I have loved you, so you also should love one another. This is how all will know that you are my disciples, if you have love for one another."

Jesus showed love throughout his life and ministry as he spread God's mercy and compassion. As we strive to be holy, to be "become like God," we must be more like Love.

CR

TO PONDER

Am I growing in the virtue of love in my life and ministry?

How do I cultivate a spirit of love in the workplace?

How can I find the balance between work and worship while still showing love to my family, friends, co-workers?

Are there people I find difficult to love? What can I do to love my "enemy"?

4

THE DAY THE ZOOM LINKS
DIED AND OTHER STORIES

FORTITUDE AND COURAGE

"Behold, new things have come."

— 2 Corinthians 5:17

"We've always done it this way."

That's a depressing sentence! It stymies change, boxes us in, keeps us from doing new things, even tries to shut down the Holy Spirit. In parish ministry, you have probably run into resistance to change, or you may resist it yourself, knowing that transitions mean a lot of work and plenty of complaints. We all need a big supply of virtue when it's time to do something differently.

For instance, there was the year that our Parish School of Religion decided to offer Zoom classes as an option. I told the Director of Religious Education that I would help set up the meetings. So, I logged in, created meetings for various classes, and basically thought I had all my ducks in a row. Wrong! My ducks were completely disheveled. When the teachers logged in, I realized I had four people trying to run meetings at the same time on one account. It simply wouldn't work that way. I think of it as the day the Zoom links died.

I had to reverse course, send apologies, work on my Zoom-ability, and regroup. After exploring how to make it work, how to add (and pay for) alternate hosts, etc., I had a system that seemed ready to go. It took the virtue of fortitude and the practice of patience from all of us — teachers, parents, students, and the Zoom team— not to throw up our hands and run away. And it took fortitude and some self-knowledge (a key ingredient in good leadership!) not to beat myself up or blame the Zoom czars. After all, I realized it was all part of the learning curve as we navigated a new, virtual landscape.

The important thing was this: We did not give up. We exercised fortitude instead. According to the *Catechism*, fortitude is "The moral virtue that ensures firmness in difficulties and constancy in the pursuit of the good. It strengthens the resolve to

resist temptations and to overcome obstacles in the moral life."
(1808)

And what can we learn from the gift and virtue of fortitude?
As Pope Francis said in a general audience in May 2014:

> In our everyday lives the Holy Spirit also makes us feel
> the closeness of the Lord, sustains us and fortifies in the
> fatigues and trials of life, so that we won't be led into
> the temptation of discouragement. ... But for all of this
> to be a reality, it is necessary that humility of heart be
> united to the gift of fortitude.

Two things here: First, it is the Holy Spirit who fortifies us in
the "fatigues and trials of life." Fortitude is given freely if we open
ourselves to the Spirit. I find that when I try to get through difficult situations at work or in life, I teeter on the verge of discour-
agement and despair, until I take it to prayer. Prayer opens the
door and lets the Holy Spirit walk in and do God's work. When
my Zoom links died, I had to go to the Lord and say: "Come on
in, I need some help!" He led me to the supply closet of virtue
and handed me some fortitude.

Second, as the pope tells us, "humility of heart" must be united to fortitude. In fact, it seems that humility must be united to
all of the virtues, because, once again, it is humility that helps us
to take God's hand and accept the graces offered to us.

On the other side of the Zoom links, there was also mercy, the kind of mercy we all need, a mercy that is compassion in action. I know the teachers must have been frustrated with me and our bad Zoom situation; I am sure the parents and students also wondered what was going on. However, they were merciful, they were patient, and for that I gave thanks.

I gave thanks, also, that once our Zoom classes worked, the DRE and staff told stories of how teachers and students were learning to interact well online. In the face of adversity, they found a connection and fostered communion. Perhaps their homes became sacred spaces; perhaps their computers/iPads/smartphones became devices that brought them into an encounter with the Holy.

Because fortitude is a cardinal virtue, other virtues flow from it. As mentioned above, it took fortitude and the power of patience to endure the setbacks of Zoom life. Another virtue that flows from fortitude is courage, which is crucial in helping us face the inevitable trials in parish life. "Courage means being able to overcome fear in order to pursue the greater good. This is not the same as being fearless; quite the contrary, the fearless person can never be truly brave."[*]

In other words, courage means taking a risk, especially if you're afraid of the consequences. You can probably think of many situations where courage is needed in ministry. Here's an

---

[*] "Fortitude," Catholic News Agency, https://www.catholicnewsagency.com/resource/55557/fortitude.

example from my parish. Recently, we began exploring a new model of faith formation involving the whole family. We have never done it this way, but both the Adult Formation director and our Parish School of Religion director kept hearing about parishes that had implemented family-based formation. From all accounts, this model was a game-changer, in a good way. They got the youth minister on board, and our religious education leaders were fired up! And somewhat afraid.

What if parishioners didn't like it? What if it didn't work? In the end, the pastor and parish leadership agreed that it was a good time to make a change. After the pastor received approval from the archbishop, we were ready to move forward, armed with courage and plenty of work to be done. Are there fears? Yes. Will it work? If we plan well and put in the effort, it will work to the best of our ability. Will some people complain? No doubt. Will we put it in God's hands? Definitely.

This is a simple example. I know many in other parishes who have had to have the courage to deal with difficult issues, to tell the truth to those in charge. I know brave parish staff members and volunteers who speak up because they love their priests, their parishes, and their Lord; they have courage to do what is right for the good of Christ and his Church. I know priests, as well, who have had the courage to make bold changes for the good of the church. In parish ministry, we all need to have both fortitude, patience, and courage at hand; we need to stand up for our faith, persevere in doing what is right, and live the way of Jesus, who reminds us: "Blessed are those who hunger and thirst for righteousness."

It takes fortitude and courage to live all the beatitudes, even when working in a Catholic context. But, as a wise friend reminded me: We have to be careful that we don't leave Jesus out of things. This parish is his, this ministry is his. Take heart, stock up on some fortitude and let it blossom into the courage you'll need.

ଔ

Virtue: Fortitude/Courage
As Lived and Taught by Jesus: Matthew 23:23–26
All throughout the Gospels, Jesus challenges authority. He cures on the Sabbath, cleanses the Temple, speaks to women, and gives a litany of woes to the Pharisees. He speaks the truth. He has courage. Just a sampling:

> Woe to you, scribes and Pharisees, you hypocrites. You pay tithes of mint and dill and cummin, and have neglected the weightier things of the law: judgment and mercy and fidelity. [But] these you should have done, without neglecting the others. Blind guides, who strain out the gnat and swallow the camel! Woe to you, scribes and Pharisees, you hypocrites. You cleanse the outside

of cup and dish, but inside they are full of plunder and self-indulgence. Blind Pharisee, cleanse first the inside of the cup, so that the outside also may be clean.

Jesus came to show the world a new way. Let's have the courage to follow his lead.

CR

TO PONDER

When have I needed fortitude, firmness, in the face of difficulties? How did I handle the situation?

How do I react when things don't go as planned? Do I have the courage to think and act as Jesus would?

When have I had the courage to speak up to a colleague or clergy member, even when I feared possible repercussions?

Who do I see as an example of courage in the Church?

5

HAVE A GOOD WEEKEND AND TRY TO RELAX

EUTRAPELIA

*"Come away by yourselves to a deserted
place and rest a while."*

— Mark 6:31

"Try to relax." Those are the three little words my pastor tells me when I say I'm going to take a day off or even go away for the weekend instead of obsessively checking that everything is in place for Sunday Masses.

He says, "Try to relax," because he knows I'm not very good at it. After all, I am dedicated to my job because I love my parish.

I hope you love yours, too! But sometimes, we must admit, it can be overwhelming and exhausting. Sure, there are days when the parish office is fairly quiet and the work mundane; other days may go something like this:

You arrive at 8:00 a.m. and are told the air conditioner in meeting room 2 isn't working. You start to text the maintenance person about the AC when someone else walks in to tell you the table setup is wrong in meeting room 11 and asks why can't that be solved? You're attending to that issue when the phone rings. The funeral home wants to arrange a funeral for someone on Wednesday, but you have to make sure the school program is over in time for a funeral in church. And then someone arrives hoping to schedule five Masses for four people, with specific date requests and wants to take the cards home, so no, you can't do it later. Plus, you suddenly realize to your great dismay that it's almost time to submit the bulletin, but the internet is down! And wait: Where is the money bag from the 6:00 p.m. Mass, the counters ask?

It's only 9:00 a.m., and you've just juggled a litany of issues. Not that you can't handle it all; in fact, I know you can! But this non-stop settling of needs and addressing of every issue under the sun builds up over time. You try to stay focused on the fact that you are loving and serving the Lord through the people you encounter. But you are only human, even in your effort to be more like God. Sometimes you just need to get away. Sometimes you really do need to relax.

How do you know when that time has come? Clue No. 1: You

wake up and think: "It's a beautiful day for a walk, but I should get to work early to get things done before the workday starts." Clue No. 2: You burst into tears when someone asks you why the tidbit about the dinner thing didn't get into the bulletin. Clue No. 3: You get to work at 8:00 a.m. and leave at 6:00 p.m. and wonder: Where did the day go? I didn't even get to the checklist. I was too busy counting tables, finding money bags, answering questions about why a holy day of obligation isn't a holy day of obligation on a Monday, making signs for two meetings that switched rooms, and dealing with a mysterious delivery from the UPS man that included an eagle's head costume (which I finally figured out was meant for the public school across the street).

On days like that it might be good to remember: When the going gets tough, the tough need to get going — and by "going" I mean "away." Getting away is a good way to stay emotionally healthy. And it doesn't always mean taking a weeklong trip — who can afford that anyway? Sometimes it means simply taking a walk, getting up from your desk for a moment and sitting outside or pulling up your favorite playlist and having a cup of tea.

Finally, "getting away" also means making time for relaxation in the very heart of your work. Did Jesus seem overburdened and stressed in his ministry? Or did he commend Mary, who had "chosen the better part"? We are, like Martha, often anxious and worried about many things. In fact, most of us are professional Marthas — serving, managing, emailing, moving boxes, arranging meetings, dealing with overflowing toilets; you name it, we have to do it! But our hearts need to maintain that focus at the feet of Jesus, to be open to his Word and let ourselves rest in his presence. Keeping our focus on the one thing can help us to do the many things with great love and peace. It can also help us heed my pastor's advice: Try to relax.

In thinking about relaxation, I ran across a virtue that is rarely discussed, hard to pronounce, and sorely needed: *Eutrapelia*.

Its name comes from the Greek, and Aristotle speaks of it as "wittiness" or the "right turn of phrase" or "deeds to achieve a good." Related to playfulness and good-natured fun, it's the simple joy that enlivens company and warms the heart. It also refers to the well-earned relaxation after a prolonged effort and the fulfillment of a weighty duty. Eutrapelia is honorable and cheerful and leads us into her dance.*

None other than St. Thomas Aquinas spoke of the virtue of eutrapelia in his *Summa Theologiae*:

Consequently, the remedy for weariness of soul must needs consist in the application of some pleasure ...

---

* Jean Francois Thomas, "The Forgotten Virtue of Eutrapelia," *Aletia*, October 16, 2020, https://aleteia.org/2020/10/16/the-forgotten-virtue-of-eutrapelia/

man's mind would break if its tension were never relaxed. Now such like words or deeds wherein nothing further is sought than the soul's delight, are called playful or humorous. Hence it is necessary at times to make use of them, in order to give rest, as it were, to the soul.

Body and soul need to relax. We will break from the tension if we don't take a break from the work. So, yes, a walk, a trip, your favorite music. Of course, the very best way to exercise eutrapelia is by honoring the Lord's Day. Don't let Sunday be like any other day. It should be set aside to, well, honor the Lord. It's a day to relax and appreciate all that God has done for us.

Relaxing body and mind is just as crucial as getting your checklist done. It is crucial so that we can detach ourselves from the things of this world and put God first in our lives. If we aren't connected to the Source, how can we juggle the jillion things on our plate with a smile? The simple answer: We can't.

So dig through the supply closet and let yourself enjoy a little eutrapelia, especially on the Lord's Day. Enjoy the wonders of the sunlight glinting on a lake, the smile of a child, the warmth of a crackling fire on a cold winter's day.

Try to relax. After all, even God rested. Eutrapelia invites us to follow his lead and enter into the dance.

⋈

Virtue: Eutrapelia
As Lived and Taught by Jesus: Mt 8:23–26

Did Jesus take time to relax? Did he practice eutrapelia? I think so. Sometimes he did that by joining people for a meal, or by withdrawing to pray. For me, one of the greatest examples of Jesus relaxing amid the chaos is this:

> He got into a boat and his disciples followed him. Suddenly a violent storm came up on the sea, so that the boat was being swamped by waves; but he was asleep. They came and woke him, saying, "Lord, save us! We are perishing!" He said to them, "Why are you terrified, O you of little faith?" Then he got up, rebuked the winds and the sea, and there was great calm.

I think there can be a tendency to think of Jesus as a man on a mission — and he was! — but the mission was to transform lives by revealing God's love and mercy. Relax, and you've got this!

CR

TO PONDER

When do I notice myself feeling overwhelmed at work? What steps do I take to relax amid the chaos?

How can I give myself time to simply "be" and not always "do"?

How can I balance contemplation and action during the work-day?

Have people told me to relax lately? Is there something I'm not seeing about the level of tension in my life?

6

THE CHRISTMAS OF MANY MASSES

GENTLENESS

*"A slave of the Lord should not quarrel,
but should be gentle with everyone."*
— 2 Timothy 2:24

Every year for as long as I can remember, we had two Masses at 4:00 p.m. on Christmas Eve: one in the church and one in the cafeteria. Regardless, it was still standing room only at both.

Over lunch in the office one day not long before Christmas, someone mentioned that it would be nice if we could accommodate even more people at 4:00 p.m. The discussion continued and grew, and before we knew it, we had decided to add a *third* 4:00 p.m. Mass, this one in the "old church," now a parish hall. We have a pastor, pa-

51

rochial vicar, and retired priest available, so why not?

We immediately started a checklist (I love lists!): Rent chairs, count ciboria, find another Nativity set, arrange for music, recruit ushers, etc. Best of all, we decided not to advertise this Mass. Instead, it would be a Christmas surprise to those who would have been left standing in the back of church, elbow to elbow with young and old in their Christmas best.

Speaking of Christmas best, we once had some complaints about too many poinsettias. Our church was a sea of poinsettias surrounding a new Nativity set. The plants in church were arranged lovingly by a team of volunteers, and thanks to the enormous talent of one of our staff members, even our Parish Center and Cafeteria Masses were made beautiful. They became fitting places to celebrate and encounter the Word-made-flesh.

So why the complaints? Certainly we spent some money on the extra poinsettias. But what was our purpose? We wanted to celebrate the great gift of God's presence with us with beauty. As St. John Paul II said in his 1999 *Letter to Artists*, quoting the author Dostoyevsky: "Beauty will save the world" (16).

It is likely that neither the pope nor Dostoyevsky had poinsettia arrangements in mind when talking about beauty, and maybe our poinsettias didn't save the world. But they did lift the spirits of most of our parishioners, especially those whose spirits sorely needed to be lifted. In fact, on the other side of the complaints, I heard people say they were in tears walking into our church for Christmas; others said that they didn't expect Mass in the cafeteria to be so meaningful, so full of light and love.

And isn't that the point of celebrating Christmas: to celebrate God's beauty and love? Christmas is full of wonder and awe. Of course, when you are on the providing side of things, when you are busy preparing for the Christmas of many Masses, it can be tricky. To be honest, I was in danger of losing focus on the wonder and awe, that is, until I ran into a door frame.

Rushing down a school hallway to put something where it needed to be and answering a text about Mass times instead of watching where I was headed, I ran smack dab into a metal doorway. I got a nasty black eye and some first aid. But not long after applying an ice pack, I answered a call that started with an anxious young woman yelling at me. That led to a meltdown in the middle of the church (with no one there — just Jesus, me, and the security cameras).

Sometimes God has to hit me over the head, quite literally. In that moment, in tears in the middle of the empty church, with a giant knot on my forehead and my eye a shiny black and blue, I heard God whisper to my heart: *Slow down. Be patient. Be gentle with yourself. I am here with you always.*

My momentary meltdown helped me pause and ponder the magnificent mystery of it all. In my impatience to get everything done, had I lost sight of what I was doing? I sat there and was reminded of a poem that I read years ago by John Shea called "Sharon's Christmas Prayer." It's a poem that points to the way we should think about Christmas, especially the Christmas of many Masses:

> She was five
> sure of the facts
> and recited them
> with slow solemnity
> convinced every word
> was revelation.
> She said
> they were so poor
> they had only peanut butter and jelly sandwiches
> to eat
> and they went a long way from home
> without getting lost. The lady rode
> a donkey, the man walked, and the baby
> was inside the lady.
>
> They had to stay in a stable
> with an ox and an ass (hee-hee)
> but the Three Rich Men found them
> because a star lit the roof.
> Shepherds came and you could
> pet the sheep but not feed them.
>
> Then the baby was borned.

And do you know who he was?
Her quarter eyes inflated
to silver dollars.

The baby was God.

And she jumped in the air,
whirled round, dove into the sofa,
and buried her head under a cushion
which is the only proper response
to the Good News of the Incarnation.[*]

God comes to us, right into our mess, black eyes and all, and asks nothing but that we love him. Maybe we need to jump up from our complacency, pause from our checklist of things to do, whirl around, and either bury our heads under the cushions for a moment because of the sheer magnificence of it all or shout it from the rooftops.

We should also, God knows, be patient and gentle with ourselves, for God came to us in the gentlest form we can imagine.

☙

---

[*] © John Shea, used by permission, "The Real Christmas Story," December 18, 1989, https://ronrolheiser.com/the-real-christmas-story/

Virtue: Gentleness

As Lived and Taught by Jesus: Matthew 11:28–30

If we fail to accept the gentle embrace of Jesus, parish work can be depleting rather than fulfilling. Jesus invites us to let him carry our load.

> Come to me, all you who labor and are burdened, and I will give you rest. Take my yoke upon you and learn from me, for I am meek and humble of heart; and you will find rest for yourselves. For my yoke is easy, and my burden light.

If we accept the virtue of gentleness and keep it ever handy, it can make all the difference both to us and to all we hope to serve.

ॐ

TO PONDER

How do you refocus when the busyness of parish life, especially in preparing for holidays, threatens to get in the way?

What role does beauty play in leading us to God?

How can you let the gentle Jesus guide you in times of stress?

Do you find it easier to be gentle with others or with yourself? Why?

7

IN HONOR OF SAINT MEINRAD

HOSPITALITY

*"Do not neglect hospitality, for through it some
have unknowingly entertained angels."*
— Hebrews 13:2

My father's name was Meinrad, named after his father, who no doubt was named after Saint Meinrad's Archabbey in Indiana, not too far from where they lived. Growing up, I was very curious about this odd name. Eventually, I discovered that Saint Meinrad is known as the martyr of hospitality, because the German Benedictine monk's hospitality to those who visited him eventually cost him his life: "In 861, two robbers came to Meinrad's hermitage, believing he had treasures hidden there … In spite of a premonition of his impending death, Meinrad invited the robbers in and offered them food and drink. The men murdered him and then fled in fear."*

Meinrad's story reminds me that the virtue of hospitality is vital in parish life. In fact, the Rule of St. Benedict puts it this way: "All guests who present themselves are to be welcomed as Christ, for he himself will say: I was a stranger and you welcomed me (Mt 25:35)."

It also reminds me that Christian hospitality does not come without cost. Will people take advantage of our hospitality? No doubt. We do it anyway. Why? Because we follow the way of Jesus. He welcomed everyone. Jesus shows us that God is a hospitable Father. Our response is to be hospitable to others, to make room for anyone who crosses our path. When a stranger walks into the parish office, we are called to greet him or her as we would greet Jesus, no matter the clothes they wear or the attitudes they bring.

Will we sometimes get burned? Absolutely. Consider this story:

A young man stopped by our parish office one day to ask for food and tell us how he had been biking across the country looking for a community that cares. He had some holes in his story, that's for sure, but the receptionist told him he could get some food out of our donation box. He did that, but then he went out-

---

* "Life of St. Meinrad," St. Meinrad Archabbey, https://www.saintmeinrad.org/the-monastery/history/life-of-st-meinrad/.

side and took the parochial vicar's bike for a ride. She told him he had to get off and come back inside. He became combative, especially when we told him he had to finish up and go because the school children were about to come into the building. Suspicious of this character and with a premonition he might come back, the receptionist called me at a church meeting that night and suggested I lock the bike up inside the office. I did so, but when I got to work the next morning, the bike was gone.

Checking the security cameras, I saw the man in question return and try to open all of the doors without success; I kept watching and then I saw him stroll across the parish office foyer, take the bike and walk out the door. How did he get in, I wondered? Walking outside, I saw that a screen had been cut. He had just crawled in through a window (which I confess was not locked.).

I filed a police report, but the pastor's response when I told him what had happened was this: "He must have needed that bike more than we did. God bless him. I will pray for him."

We showed hospitality, we exercised kindness and compassion, and our bike was stolen. Do we offer condemnation and judgment? Not according to our pastor, who showed us how to put on the mind of Christ. Always, we offer just mercy. Just compassion. In a sense, we are called to be martyrs of hospitality. (Not literally, we hope!)

Another story of hospitality ends on a sweeter note. For a

year or so, there was a gentleman who came to Mass every day. He walked down a path behind our church, and when he arrived, he sat in the back and prayed. He looked a bit disheveled, and we weren't sure what his story was. But he was there, every day. Our daily communicants knew his name and considered him part of our parish family.

One day, a school parent talked to the pastor about the man who hung out outside our church. Fearful, she wanted something done about him. Of course, nothing was "done." In fact, the following Holy Thursday, the gentleman had his feet washed by the pastor. Eventually, our friend moved away. We hope that we offered him the hospitality he needed to live his faith.

Our homes, our offices, our lives should always make for a hospitable place for others to encounter God. I recently visited a friend whose house was not only neat and orderly, but serene and prayerful. I felt at home there, I felt the presence of God. She had turned her home into a hospitable place for the Holy Spirit to reside.

In the parish office, we should try to do the same, and it all starts with being attentive, with remembering where we are and what we are here to do: Be the face of Christ to others.

A few years ago, I named the area around our reception desk the "zone of positivity." No gossip was allowed, no negativity would be endured. It was somewhat of a joke, but it shouldn't be. Maybe now we should call the whole parish office the "Zone of Hospitality" so that we always remember to make room for others to encounter Christ.

CR

Virtue: Hospitality
As Lived and Taught by Jesus: Matthew 14:15–21
In the feeding of the multitudes, a miracle so important that it appears in all four Gospels, and twice in two of them, it's important to note that Jesus does not send people away:

> When it was evening, the disciples approached him and said, "This is a deserted place and it is already late; dismiss the crowds so that they can go to the villages and buy food for themselves." Jesus said to them, "There is no need for them to go away; give them some food yourselves." But they said to him, "Five loaves and two fish are all we have here." Then he said, "Bring them here to me," and he ordered the crowds to sit down on the grass. Taking the five loaves and the two fish, and looking up to heaven, he said the blessing, broke the loaves, and gave them to the disciples, who in turn gave them to the crowds. They all ate and were satisfied, and they picked up the fragments left over — twelve wicker baskets full.

Feed them yourselves, Jesus says. And if you feel you don't have enough, if you are too tired, give what you have to God; he will supply the rest.

CR

TO PONDER

How do I practice hospitality in my parish work?

When is hospitality a challenge?

How does the life of Jesus help me to show hospitality?

How can I help spread the spirit of hospitality in our parish?

8

FULLY, CONSCIOUSLY, AND FORGETFULLY

GRATITUDE

*"Let the word of Christ dwell in you richly, as
in all wisdom you teach and admonish one
another, singing psalms, hymns, and spiritual
songs with gratitude in your hearts to God."*
— Colossians 3:16

You don't know what you've got till it's gone. Although I do
hope the pandemic of 2020–22 is a distant memory now, it
brought that hackneyed but honest sentiment to life for me and
many others. To illustrate that, here's a story I like to call "fully,

consciously, and forgetfully."

When we were live-streaming Mass from an empty church in spring of 2020, the pastor and parochial vicar usually celebrated Mass together, with the concelebrant doing the readings and responses. One day, when the parochial vicar was away, the pastor asked me to read and wear a wireless microphone for the responses. In other words, I was the congregation. Yikes! I got through the readings just fine, but when it came time to respond to the Invitation to Prayer, when we are supposed to say "May the Lord accept the sacrifice at your hands ... " I completely blanked out. The pastor had to rescue me.

I had thought I had things under control. After all, how many times had I been to Mass in my lifetime? But in the moment, I quickly realized that frequency doesn't matter, but also how much we depend upon one another as a community of faith. There is such power in our presence together, and that awkward experience reminded me of how my role was both insignificant and very significant at the same time. I prepared a handy "cheat sheet" for next time. But when the next time came around, I was able to remember that I was not alone. There were many members of our parish family connected at home, watching the live stream. It also helped me to recall what Vatican II taught in its Constitution on the Sacred Liturgy: The Church "earnestly desires that all the faithful should be led to that fully conscious and active participation in liturgical celebrations which is demanded by the very nature of the liturgy. Such participation by the Christian people as 'a chosen race, a royal priesthood, a holy nation, a redeemed people (1 Pt 2:9; cf. 2:4-5), is their right and duty by reason of their baptism'" (14).

Despite the way it seemed, with our camera controls and livestreaming studio (aka the vesting sacristy), the Mass is neither a show nor a production, but the highest form of worship, a "foretaste of that heavenly liturgy" (*SC*, 8). Or, as Pope Benedict XVI pointed out in *The Spirit of the Liturgy*: "The real 'action' in the liturgy in which we are all supposed to participate is the action of God himself."

In liturgy, we worship the God who created us, came to us, died for us, rose for us, and remains with us always. To be prepared to enter into the divine action, we need to be reverent and ready to meet God at Mass, whether we carry the words on a cheat sheet or can recite them by heart, whether we are watching from home (hopefully in a sacred space) or participating from the pew. Whatever the case, worship is God's great invitation to be with him on holy ground.

The experience that made me cringe reminded me of my right and my duty. It reminded me, also, that

- I am not in control.
- I am not alone.
- I should be ready to enter into the Lord's presence.
- I should remember to have gratitude for the power of people gathered to worship.

The next time I was the congregation at Mass, with wireless

mic and cheat sheet ready for the people's responses, I nearly broke down reading from the Acts of the Apostles. I don't really know why — but the Spirit moved me. God took the opportunity to remind me who was running the show. Afterward, I got several calls and texts from parishioners just wanting to check in on me. We are not alone, not when we are connected as the Body of Christ, whether in person or not. We are here with and for the Lord. As Pope Benedict XVI wrote, "God himself acts and does what is essential. He inaugurates the new creation, makes himself accessible to us, so that through the things of the earth, through our gifts, we can communicate with him in a personal way."

Isn't that beautiful? Who wouldn't want to communicate with God in a personal way?

As our congregation moved back into the church, I remembered my days as a congregation of one and was relieved those days were behind me. I was humbled to have been able to attend the liturgy on behalf of so many who longed to receive the Eucharist. But when our pews began to fill up, I was filled with gratitude to see my brothers and sisters. I thought about how we all come from different places, how we all live different stories and bring them to this church, how we all come to worship our God carrying joys and burdens, hopes and heartaches. We are people of faith, strained or thriving, with hearts full of love or fear, joy or sadness. But we come here to worship our God and partake of his great gift, the gift of himself.

I have no doubt that my newfound gratitude for gathering as the people of God to celebrate the Eucharist was also felt by many who hungered not only to be together but to receive the Eucharist. The Eucharist is, after all, "a sacrifice of thanksgiving to the Father, a blessing by which the Church expresses her gratitude to God for all his benefits, for all that he has accomplished through creation, redemption, and sanctification. Eucharist means first of all 'thanksgiving.'" (CCC 1360)

It is our right and duty, our blessing and privilege, to gather for the Eucharist, to respond to God's generosity with grateful hearts. Perhaps this time in parish life will bring a newfound gratitude both for gathering as a community and for the Eucharist at the center of it all.

Stocking up on gratitude for the Eucharist and this family of faith is a lesson I need to remember. "Grateful people do not claim things as their own, but cherish everything as given and received. Yet gratitude is elusive. We are grateful for a while, and then we forget. It is a virtue that needs attention."*

ଓ

Virtue: Gratitude
As Lived and Taught by Jesus: Luke 7:44–48
One of my favorite passages in the Gospels is the Pardon of the Sinful Woman in the Gospel of Luke. Why my favorite? Probably be-

---

* Jerry Fagin, S.J., *Putting on the Heart of Christ* (Chicago: Loyola Press, 2010).

cause I think she might be me and I might be her. To be forgiven, to feel God's mercy, is a life-changing experience that engenders gratitude. God showers so much love upon us when we go to him with our tears, with our joys, with our very selves. This passage shows us that outpouring of gratitude.

> Then he turned to the woman and said to Simon, "Do you see this woman? When I entered your house, you did not give me water for my feet, but she has bathed them with her tears and wiped them with her hair. You did not give me a kiss, but she has not ceased kissing my feet since the time I entered. You did not anoint my head with oil, but she anointed my feet with ointment. So I tell you, her many sins have been forgiven; hence, she has shown great love. But the one to whom little is forgiven, loves little."

God's abundant mercy and forgiveness prompt us to show great love, to anoint the feet of Jesus with our tears, our joys, and our ministry to his Church. It also reminds us to be grateful, to forgive as we have been forgiven.

℘

TO PONDER

What am I most grateful for in my work life? My family life?

How do I connect gratitude to the Eucharist?

How can I give thanks to God by showing love to others?

Do I remember to give thanks to God each day for things large and small?

9

FOUR FEET SHORT WITH FIVE MINUTES TO GO

PRUDENCE

"I, Wisdom, dwell with prudence,
and useful knowledge I have."
— Proverbs 8:12

What's the most wonderful time of the year? There's a song that may convince you that the answer is Christmas — a wonderful celebration, indeed! However, for our Catholic Faith, Easter is the most important of all liturgical times. And the Sacred Triduum leading to Easter is a time set aside, a time to encounter Jesus Christ in a profound way.

Of course, if you work in a parish office, Holy Week and Easter are a test of all the virtues. Be patient, show mercy, have fortitude! Be organized! Did you change the church colors from purple to red to purple to white to red to white? Did you order the right size paschal candle and inspect it when it arrived just in case it broke in two during shipment (as it did for us one year!)?

The first year I worked in the parish office, I ordered a thirty-six-inch paschal candle. I had to pray it through the year, as I watched it shrink through funerals and baptisms until it was a tiny paschal candle. I ended up naming it "The Little Candle that Could" because it made it all the way until the next Easter. Barely.

But I digress.

I love the Triduum, and I love Easter. But you must be ready to expect the unexpected and respond accordingly. (One Holy Thursday, someone shipped live lobsters to the pastor. "Take care of that box," the FedEx man said. "There's something alive in there." The pastor still refers to the people who sent that package as "my lobster friends.")

Now back to the story I wanted to share.

One Holy Thursday a few years ago, I was in the narthex about five minutes before Mass. The pastor called me over and whispered: "I need you to find two people for washing the feet." Two residents from a local senior center had been scheduled to be part of our twelve-person lineup. However, the bus that was supposed to bring them hadn't shown up.

So off I went to find four feet, with five minutes to go. It wasn't hard, really. I just had to scan the crowd (in a hurry!) to consider who might be willing to take part. I also had to think about how to phrase the invitation so it didn't sound like: "Hey, someone didn't show up, can we have your feet?"

I found two volunteers quickly, with no questions asked, and gave thanks, as I often do, for our generous parishioners. I also gave thanks for my pastor, who trusted me to take care of what we needed in five minutes flat. As long as we do things for the glory of God, it all can be done.

Later, I reflected on two things.

First, what virtue was needed to take on such a task in a hurry? Prudence came to mind.

"Prudence is the first of the cardinal virtues because it is the ability to look at a concrete situation and know what ought to be done. It is the ability to make right judgments."*

Prudence helps us look at a situation and respond to it "right." In this instance, it was not hard to be prudent. It helped tremendously that I knew seventy-five percent of the congregation. That's how I knew whom to ask and who might be offended by — or nervous about — the last-minute invitation.

Other challenges are more complex and require extra-large prudence. For instance, who gets the Easter hydrangeas? (We'll

---

* "Prudence," Catholic News Agency, https://www.catholicnewsagency.com/resource/55554/prudence.

get back to that in a minute.)

My second point about Holy Thursday is that I had to make sure my last-minute task didn't distract me (or anyone else) from the beauty of the liturgy. The Mass of the Lord's Supper is deep, it is a "thin place" where you can encounter God powerfully. In fact, I had never been to Mass on Holy Thursday until I went through RCIA at the age of forty-two, and it changed my life (which needed some changing). The power of the music, the Sacrament, the lighting all came together and had a powerful impact on me. I was changed. I remember calling my mother the next morning and asking: "Why didn't you ever take us to Mass on Holy Thursday?" Too many small children, she said. She had a point.

Anyway, as I said, I couldn't let my job overshadow this opportunity to be present to the Lord Jesus. The Mass celebrates the institution of the Eucharist, the institution of the priesthood, and gives us the model of how to serve others as Jesus did. In the washing of the feet, parishioners from all backgrounds make themselves vulnerable; they sit and let the priest wash and kiss their feet. They sit there for all of us, representing our parish family. The priest, meanwhile, shows us what love looks like. As the great spiritual writer Henri Nouwen observed, in the washing of the feet, "Jesus calls us to continue his mission of revealing the perfect love of God in this world." Revealing God's love in the world. That seems like a prudent thing to do. Nothing we do in this world should be for our own gain, but all for the glory of God.

Meanwhile, back to the hydrangeas. Not even two weeks into the Easter season, we have parishioners calling wanting to take our beautiful pink and blue hydrangeas home. The problem is: How do we decide who gets hydrangeas and who doesn't? The prudent thing to do was this: We decided to keep them every Easter and plant them around our campus. But first, we needed to find a hydrangea hiding place. All in a day's work!

℞

Virtue: Prudence

As Lived and Taught by Jesus: Mark 12:13–17

In pondering the scriptures and what Jesus teaches us about prudence, I recalled that there were many who were always trying to trap and trick Jesus. He would have none of it. He teaches us a great lesson in prudence:

> They sent some Pharisees and Herodians to him to en-snare him in his speech. They came and said to him, "Teacher, we know that you are a truthful man and that you are not concerned with anyone's opinion. You do not regard a person's status but teach the way of God in accordance with the truth. Is it lawful to pay the census tax to Caesar or not? Should we pay or should we not

pay?" Knowing their hypocrisy he said to them, "Why are you testing me? Bring me a denarius to look at." They brought one to him and he said to them, "Whose image and inscription is this?" They replied to him, "Caesar's." So Jesus said to them, "Repay to Caesar what belongs to Caesar and to God what belongs to God." They were utterly amazed at him.

Real prudence turns the tables on the no-win situations we encounter. With prudence, we are often able to sidestep the things that can trip us up in parish ministry.

CR

TO PONDER

When have I needed the virtue of prudence?

How do I use prudence when having to make last-minute decisions? Or any decisions?

What does the life and ministry of Jesus teach me about prudence?

How can I develop the virtue of prudence?

10

TAKE THAT LOG OUT OF YOUR EYE AND HAVE A GOOD LAUGH

HUMOR

"Then our mouths were filled with laughter;
our tongues sang for joy.
Then it was said among the nations,
'The Lord had done great things for them.'"
— Psalm 126:2

Children read and hear the Gospels with fresh eyes and ears. Maybe that's why Jesus said we must become like little children to enter the kingdom of heaven. Children haven't been lulled into a sense of complacency like those of us who have heard the Gospel stories for decades; we have heard them so often that many of us have become numb to their power.

Perhaps we have also been deadened to the fact that there are underpinnings of humor in the Gospels. When I was young, I remember being struck by this image: "How can you say to your brother, 'Let me remove that splinter from your eye,' while the wooden beam is in your eye?" (Mt 7:4). A wooden beam in your eye? That was too funny, I thought. It was also a very powerful image. Even as a child, I knew what Jesus was saying: Do not judge others when you have your own mess — an even bigger mess — to deal with. I imagined the beam hanging out of my eye because I had been mad at my sister for a something small, when I was well aware I had lost her favorite doll.

So yes, I thought that log in the eye was pretty funny, but that image taught me a lesson I still remember. A sense of humor, by way of an ability to laugh at ourselves (not laugh at others), is a Christian virtue, a path to holiness. In the time of Jesus, it's no doubt that many of his stories and parables may have elicited a smile or a laugh while also making a powerful point. A healthy sense of humor can be a great asset in ministry. As Fr. Romano Guardini once put it: "One other thing is required by kindness, something of which we rarely speak — a sense of humor. It helps us to endure things more easily. Indeed we could hardly get along without it."

Father Guardini is right: We can hardly get along without a healthy sense of humor, wouldn't you agree? I would. I know I need to be able to laugh at myself, especially when I do things like leave the "p" out of "passed away" in an email sent to the two thousand people on our parish email list. Or the time I double-booked the church but didn't know it until a priest called to say, "We won't have a 10:00 a.m. Mass there after all." Good thing, I thought, because there are two hundred people in the church right now for a funeral!

If laughter is the best medicine, we all need a healthy dose. Agains Father Guardini: "The person who sees man only seriously, only morally or pedagogically, cannot endure him for any great length of time. We must have an eye for the oddity of existence. ... A friendly laugh at the oddity of all human affairs — that is humor."

The oddity for existence is all around us, and that's why we need to be able to laugh, mostly at ourselves!

Why is humor important? Principally because it keeps us from taking ourselves too seriously. If we recognize that here on earth we have not a lasting city, it's perhaps best to laugh at the incongruities while joyfully accepting God's grace to act as agents of His redemption. In other words, perhaps a believer's best attitude in life is to change what we can change and laugh at what we cannot, completely confident that God has already bested whatever tries to keep us from joy.*

Of course, to think of a sense of humor as a virtue means that it leads us to that holiness and helps us become like God. In our world today, of course, there is a lot of non-virtuous humor. It takes prudence to recognize which sense of humor to take out of our supply closet when needed.

But truly, if we cannot laugh in this crazy life, we will surely cry. I have always admired my friend, our parish receptionist, for how she handles the strangest phone calls. There was the man who called and said, "I want to tickle your feet" and the woman who wanted to find out about a "virginization" ceremony. Our receptionist answers with kindness, equanimity, and respectful listening. And then she hangs up and we have to laugh. Or we'd have to quit.

In his apostolic exhortation *Gaudete et Exsultate* (On the Call to Holiness in Today's World), Pope Francis says this:

> Christian joy is usually accompanied by a sense of hu-
> mour. We see this clearly, for example, in Saint Thomas
> More, Saint Vincent de Paul and Saint Philip Neri. Ill
> humour is no sign of holiness. "Remove vexation from
> your mind" (*Eccl* 11:10). We receive so much from the

---

* William J. King, "On the Importance of Humor," Simply Catholic, https://www.simplycatholic.com/on-the-importance-of-humor/.

Lord "for our enjoyment" (1 Tm 6:17), that sadness can
be a sign of ingratitude. We can get so caught up in ourselves that we are unable to recognize God's gifts. (126)

Sometimes, I forget to laugh at myself, and I am tempted to get
"caught up" in my own drama. But then I remember that I'm
walking around with a great big log in my eye. It'll take awhile to
get it out. Meanwhile, I can laugh.

∽

Virtue: Sense of Humor
As Lived and Taught by Jesus: Luke 15:8–10
It may seem hard to think of Jesus as having a sense of humor.
But remember that "humor" was likely quite different in his time.
In fact, some of the Gospel stories were probably quite funny …
to his listeners. The parables, for instance, always have a surprise
ending, a "gotcha" moment. Leaving ninety-nine sheep to find
one? Hiding your light under a bushel basket? This had to make
people smile. Here's one of my favorites, not least because the
woman is an image of God — that had to be funny!

Or what woman having ten coins and losing one would
not light a lamp and sweep the house, searching careful-
ly until she finds it? And when she does find it, she calls

together her friends and neighbors and says to them, 'Rejoice with me because I have found the coin that I lost.' In just the same way, I tell you, there will be rejoicing among the angels of God over one sinner who repents.

Thank God our faith doesn't mean that we have to be somber and serious all the time. Sometimes, a good chuckle is what keeps us going.

☙

TO PONDER

How can I cultivate a sense of humor in the workplace?

What is hard about laughing at myself?

How do you see a sense of humor as a virtue?

Recall a funny story from the "trenches" of your ministry.

II

JUST BE YOURSELF

SELF-WORTH

*"My son, with humility have self-esteem;
and give yourself the esteem you deserve."*
— Sirach 10:28

I understand low self-esteem; it has been a demon I've battled off and on my whole life. Although I have to say that it was mostly *on* in my younger years and more or less *off* with flare-ups as I've grown older. Where it comes from, I don't know, but it simmers under the surface. We all have difficulties in life, crosses to bear. The battle with self-esteem is mine.

When we're working for a parish or a school or any church ministry, I think the demons get a little more pushy. As we endeavor to serve God with all of our hearts, God's nemesis is right there, trying to pull us away. It happens when I'm putting together an email or bulletin notice or scheduling events on the calendar and my mind starts to wonder. *Sure, I can do these boring things, but why can't I make beautiful bows or turn trash into treasure? Why can't I be fun and engaging instead of quiet and low key?* In other words, I often engage the question: "What's wrong with me?"

The truth is that any group is built of a variety of personalities, with a variety of life experiences, but we are all made in the image of God. And, as Saint Paul tells us, of course we all have different gifts. That's how God intends it to be. Dear Romans, Paul said:

> For as in one body we have many parts, and all the parts do not have the same function, so we, though many, are one body in Christ and individually parts of one another. Since we have gifts that differ according to the grace given to us, let us exercise them: if prophecy, in proportion to the faith; if ministry, in ministering; if one is a teacher, in teaching; if one exhorts, in exhortation; if one contributes, in generosity; if one is over others, with diligence; if one does acts of mercy, with cheerfulness. (12:4–8)

Whatever gifts we possess, whatever we do, none of it is for us anyway. We work for the glory of God, as instruments of grace for the benefit of others. If we forget that sometimes — as we are bound to do — perhaps we need to go back to the source, back to the treasure of all virtue: the Eucharist.

To sit with the Blessed Sacrament is to align our gaze with pure holiness, to realize what and who we are called to be. That is what we need to get through each day. Perhaps, when we begin to suffer from low self-esteem and self-doubt, we should remember to clothe ourselves with Christ, as St. Paul said to the Romans, and thus dress for spiritual success.

Clothing ourselves in the virtues of Christ should keep us on the right path. It should also aid us in carrying whatever cross we bear, and in waging the battle in our minds against whatever seeks to divert our gaze. To be grounded in Christ is to be assured of ourselves, assured by the fact that we carry God's image stamped on our souls.

In *Virtues for Ordinary Christians*, Fr. James Keenan, SJ, a moral theologian, sees self-esteem as a virtue because if we do not recognize God's image reflected in our very being, how do we live the life meant for us? Sometimes people — even those closest to us — do not recognize our value, and that's just part of life. Our value is not in what others think of us; our value comes from God. The important thing to remember is that we are to follow Jesus.

Nouwen, who we've quote previously, helps us in this area:

> Do not despair thinking that you cannot change yourself
> after so many years. Simply enter into the presence of Jesus
> as you are and ask him to give you a fearless heart where he
> can be with you. You cannot make yourself different. Jesus
> came to give you a new heart, a new spirit, a new mind,
> and a new body. Let him transform you by his love and so
> enable you to receive his affection in your whole being.

I can only be the person God created me to be, but I can be that person fearlessly. To wish to be otherwise, to waste time despairing of what I am not, is a sin. After all, such wishing to be different ignores God's life within me as I am, as God created me. Just like the number 13, which is often ignored but has its rightful place, we each have our place in the people of God. And so, self-esteem is not the opposite of humility; self-esteem is humility's source. They go hand in hand. Or, as Father Keenan puts it in *Virtues for Ordinary Chrisitans*: "Self-esteem is not humility, but the virtue that makes humility possible. If humility concerns how we interact with others, self-esteem pertains to how we live with ourselves. ... If humility is about public discourse, self-esteem is about interior dialogue."

It's that interior dialogue that can be our greatest asset or most distracting liability. Invite Jesus into the dialogue, wrap yourself up in virtue, and you can face whatever each day hands you.

And one more thing: Sometimes, you just need a spiritual boost. Recently, an elderly and wise priest helped me with the best confession. "I'm a mess," I said. "You don't look a mess," he answered, following up with "Do you know how much God loves you?" There was a twinkle in his eye because he knew at that moment he was God's love for me. He gave me a beautiful gift. We are all a mess, but God is right in the midst of the mess.

We all need physical and spiritual reminders of Christ's presence among us; we might assume working for the Church makes those reminders plentiful. That's not necessarily so. Make sure to seek out those reminders, to be aware of God's presence with you in every moment, every text, every email, every encounter with the people who cross your path each day. Be sure, also, to be those reminders for those around you. Sometimes you can be the walking supply closet, stocked with every virtue.

CB

Virtue: Self-Worth
As Lived and Taught by Jesus: Luke 7:33–35
Jesus is the Son of God, the Word-made-Flesh. He is also fully human. In his humanity, what does Jesus teach us about self-esteem? In reflecting upon this, I thought of the following Scripture passage:

For John the Baptist came neither eating food nor drink-

ing wine, and you said, "He is possessed by a demon."
The Son of Man came eating and drinking and you said,
"Look, he is a glutton and a drunkard, a friend of tax col-
lectors and sinners." But wisdom is vindicated by all her
children.

In this passage Jesus tells us that he knows what others say
about him — and it's not very nice! Nevertheless, he also fearlessly embraces the fullness of who he is in every circumstance.

CR

TO PONDER

Do I find myself comparing myself to others? Why? What is God
trying to tell me in those moments?

Does my inner dialogue acknowledge the gifts God has given
to me?

Do I fearlessly use my gifts in service of God and his people?

What are the things I struggle to accept in myself? Do I accept
those same things in others?

12

THE WEARY WORLD REJOICES

HOPE

*"For I know well the plans I have in mind
for you ... plans for your welfare and not for
woe, so as to give you a future of hope."*
— Jeremiah 29:11

There are some wonderful co-workers in the vineyard of the Lord outside of my own parish. What, I asked them, is the most challenging aspect of working in church ministry?

One answer speaks volumes: "I would have to say it is keeping Christ in Christmas. By that I mean it is way, way too easy to focus on the business of church and the busyness of church that Jesus just gets shoved on the back of the shelf. Then we are just left with a nasty elf plaguing us to 'go, do more, faster, get it done!'"

This sentiment was echoed by another friend in ministry who says the challenge of parish life is "to focus on spiritual attentiveness and accountability. It's easy for parish work to be seen as 'business.' It's easy to be caught up in trying to be responsive, efficient, organized, and productive. But that can easily distract from the real mission — of doing the Lord's will. And doing it with charitable cooperation rather than business efficiency."

When serving in a Catholic context, we have to remember that it should never be "business as usual." Instead, it's "business as unusual," because our work is always about the business of keeping Christ and his mission front and center. It seems obvious, but there are real challenges.

I would like to think that every parish is an oasis of peace and Christian unity, but I know it isn't so.

As someone who works in another parish told me:

Our parishes will be characterized and challenged by some things that are relatively fixed: the approach and demeanor of the pastor and clerics, the demographics, the budget, staff and personnel, etc. Sometimes accepting what is and continuing to work joyfully in whatever I can do, is a much more authentic way of serving God and serving the parish than fighting against what seems in "need of improvement."

Instead of fighting what we lack, in other words, we cling to what we have. That's the virtue that can help us "keep Christ in Christmas," the virtue that can help us remember what we are doing and why we are here, the virtue that gives us the energy to keep on going: hope.

When writing about hope, St. Thomas Aquinas noted that hope is born from the desire for something good that is "difficult but possible to attain." There is no need for hope if we can easily get what we want, but neither is there any reason to hope when what we desire is completely beyond our grasp.*

We are pilgrims on a journey toward God, and hope helps us see that while it is difficult, it is not impossible. You need a great big supply of hope to work or volunteer in a Catholic parish, school, or any ministry, to deal with the inevitable struggles, challenges, and despair for more than a year or two. The good news is there is Good News: We are never alone. Waddel adds:

Hope frees us from the intolerable burden of thinking

---

* Paul J. Waddell, "Hope: The Forgotten Virtue of Our Time," *America Magazine*, November 7, 2016, https://www.americamagazine.org/faith/2016/11/07/hope-forgotten-virtue-our-time.

that so much depends on us that we become oblivious to the blessings around us, and especially to how each day God calls us out of ourselves in order to draw others more fully to life through our kindness and goodness. For Christians, hope is a new and abundantly promising way of life characterized by joy and thanksgiving, service and generosity, hospitality and celebration, and even the wonderful freedom to fail.

The wonderful freedom to fail — I like that! We all falter and fail at times, but there is always hope. I am blessed to have a front row seat to stories of hope all around me. I see parishioners who engage in many acts of kindness and love, who face difficulties but move ahead with the virtue of hope planted deep within them. They care for the needy, comfort the sick, visit the lonely.

This generosity of spirit gives birth to hope and assures us that God has more in store than sometimes meets the eye. The *Catechism* defines hope as "the theological virtue by which we desire the kingdom of heaven and eternal life as our happiness, placing our trust in Christ's promises and relying not on our own strength, but on the help of the grace of the Holy Spirit" (1817). It is hope and the Holy Spirit that helps parish staff and volunteers to thrive, if only we keep our eyes on Jesus, the source of all virtue.

We may struggle with keeping that focus at times. But when

that happens, consider the story of Vietnamese Cardinal Francis Xavier Nguyen Van Thuan, who was a prisoner of the Communists for thirteen years, nine in solitary confinement. Instead of sinking into despair in prison, he became a beacon of hope. He made friends with his guards, smuggled out messages on scraps of paper that were later compiled into a book, *The Road of Hope*; he made his own pectoral cross out of bits of wood and wire, wearing it even after his release, until the end of his life as a symbol of hope.

In his encyclical *Spe Salvi* (On Christian Hope), Pope Benedict XVI recalls Cardinal Van Thuan's story:

> During thirteen years in jail, in a situation of seemingly utter hopelessness, the fact that he could listen and speak to God became for him an increasing power of hope, which enabled him, after his release, to become for people all over the world a witness to hope — to that great hope which does not wane even in the nights of solitude. (32)

Perhaps nights of solitude provide fertile ground for hope to grow. Perhaps it is more challenging when working every day, coordinating the parish calendar, remembering who meets where, negotiating parking lot compromise, etc. As a friend put it: "Because I am doing the work of the Lord, I can delude myself into thinking that I am in touch with the Lord and seeking his will. Time working doesn't substitute for time *with* the Lord: time in prayer; time seeking *his* will; time holding myself spiritually accountable. I can easily neglect this."

Neglecting time with the Lord is neglecting our best opportunity to cultivate hope and every other virtue. I can attest to this myself.

In our office, I usually gather everyone at noon to pray the Angelus. For the past few months, I have neglected the gathering almost every day. When the alarm goes off, everyone seems to be busy, so I pray it alone in my office. But that's no excuse! Forgetting or ignoring the Angelus is forgetting or ignoring why we are here in the first place. If we can't take two minutes to bow in prayer and give thanks for the Word-made-Flesh, then what kind of place is this, anyway?

So yes, I have been lax! But I know there are better days ahead. I have great hope.

◌঵

Virtue: Hope
As Lived and Taught by Jesus: Luke 18:35–43
Jesus shows us the fruits of hope in this passage from Luke, but the blind man shows us what it means to live the virtue of hope.

> Now as he approached Jericho a blind man was sitting by
> the roadside begging, and hearing a crowd going by, he

inquired what was happening. They told him, "Jesus of Nazareth is passing by." He shouted, "Jesus, Son of David, have pity on me!" The people walking in front rebuked him, telling him to be silent, but he kept calling out all the more, "Son of David, have pity on me!" Then Jesus stopped and ordered that he be brought to him; and when he came near, Jesus asked him, "What do you want me to do for you?" He replied, "Lord, please let me see." Jesus told him, "Have sight; your faith has saved you."

The blind man knew Jesus could cure him, and he persisted in calling out for help. He had Christian hope, a hope that does not disappoint. His faith saved him, but his hope made it happen.

CR

TO PONDER

What gives me hope?

How can I respond to challenges with the virtue of hope?

How can I improve my prayer life to cultivate hope?

How do I see hope related to faith and love?

13

"ALL OF MY GOOD STUFF, I GOT IT FROM THE BIBLE"

SURRENDER

*"There is an appointed time for everything,
and a time for every affair under the heavens."*

— Ecclesiastes 3:1

Parish ministry is fulfilling, beautiful, and challenging, all at the same time. So yes, we do need to stock up on our virtues when going to work. It also helps to clothe ourselves with Christ. And for that, it is necessary to have good role models.

I started thinking about this when I was sitting in my favorite coffee shop one rainy morning, humming along with a song playing in the background. Suddenly, or so it seemed, I realized what I was hearing: "Turn, Turn, Turn" by the Byrds, based on Ecclesiastes 3. That oldie brought me instantly back to September 28, 2012, my last day of employment at *The Times-Picayune* newspaper in New Orleans. I remember that September morning so clearly: I woke up, opened the daily readings to pray, and was stunned. The first reading was from the book of Ecclesiastes, Chapter 3: "There is an appointed time for everything, / and a time for every affair under the heavens" (3:1). I felt as if Ecclesiastes were speaking directly to me. Of course, it was; the living Word is always speaking to us. I also remembered that my Old Testament professor at Loyola had said that Ecclesiastes was the most depressing book in the Bible.

Even so, it was evident God was telling me that there is a time for everything. Apparently, it was time for me to let go. My life as a journalist was over. But more importantly, it was time for me to remember what this depressing-in-human-terms book was telling me: God is in charge of every affair under the heavens. And so, I went to the office, packed up my things, said goodbye, and was ready to see where he would lead.

That idea of letting God take the lead reminds me of one of the hardest virtues to cultivate: Surrender to the will of God. It also reminded me of one of my best teachers on the topic of surrender: Sr. Marina Aranzabal, STJ, a Teresian sister who worked in our parish for eighteen years before going home to the Lord after a battle with cancer.

Her battle was difficult, but brief. In January 2021, she danced in our office with joy after announcing she had been fully vaccinated. She played her guitar and sang happy birthday to two staff members — from six feet away, as she noted. Little more than a month later, she was diagnosed with metastatic colon cancer. By that May, she had died.

Some of the last words she said to me were, "I get weaker every day. Weaker, weaker, weaker. I am going down, down, down." She was surrendering herself to God in that weakness, I knew that much. And I knew she was doing it her way, as she always had.

Sister Marina had a way of speaking the truth, even in her sickness. When I visited her after her diagnosis, she was weak but still very much alert — alert enough to give me some tasks to do, such as use the right picture in her funeral program. I tried my best to tell her how much she meant to me, how her words of wisdom had brought comfort in the darkest times. She looked at me as only she could and seemed to brush my words off with her hands. "All my good stuff," she said, "I got it from the Bible, you know."

Yes, I know, Sister. But you always made it so clear, so simple, so life changing. I knew it was her way of telling me I would be fine. She was a source of compassion and comfort for many of us. She was the one who told me, during my dark hours of joblessness, that God would take care of me. She was the one who had always been there as my cheerleader and spiritual director, correcting what she liked to call my "crooked thinking."

So yes, my heart aches for the loss of Sister Marina. Just around the corner from my office, she was a listening ear and a wise woman. She took care of the poor, counseled the bereaved, and visited the imprisoned, including a death row inmate, and she did it "All for Jesus," as the Society of St. Teresa of Jesus formed her to do. Her last words to me left me with the assurance that she had simply surrendered to the Good Shepherd. All that she did flowed from the heart of Jesus. All her good stuff came from the Bible. Her secret is out.

It's a secret that can be put to good use for anyone laboring in the vineyard of the Lord. There is a time for everything; seasons and jobs and people come and go. Even this role I hold now in my parish is not mine; I fill it for a time and then I will be gone one day. In fact, I sometimes wonder how I will know when to let it go. The bigger and better question, however, is this: How will I live this life God has given me right now, at this moment, no matter what I am doing?

In a parish, we encounter so many people, and so many joys and sorrows every single day. We have our own desires, our own wishes, and our own thoughts about how things should be. But our main job is to surrender to God, to be his instrument, to bring, and bear love. For where there is love, there is God. It's in the Bible.

This idea of surrendering to God, who is love, seems simple! And it is simple, but it's not easy, especially when working in parish ministry. There are troubled souls (sometimes I'm one of them), confusing situations (I sometimes create them), people with challenging personalities or impossible requests (a daily occurrence), and too many strange phone calls and emails to count.

Then, of course, there is the fear of losing ourselves if we surrender to the will of God — although it is in surrendering that we find our very selves. Where in the closet do you find something to help you discover that? Here's a little something from Henri Nouwen:

> As I reflected this morning again on the story of the prodigal son and tried to experience myself in the embrace of the father, I suddenly felt a certain resistance to being embraced so fully and totally. I experienced not only a desire to be embraced, but also a fear of losing my independence. I realized that God's love is a jealous love. God wants not just a part of me, but all of me. Only when I surrender myself completely to God's love can I expect to be free from endless distractions, ready to hear the voice of love, and able to recognize my own unique call.[*]

Letting go and giving it all to God — allowing him to love us completely — can be a struggle, but it is a struggle that can change

---

[*] "Surrender Yourself Completely to God's Love," Henri Nouwen Society, January 9, 2022, https://henrinouwen.org/meditation/surrender-yourself-completely-to-gods-love/.

your life and the way you minister in God's church. If you don't believe Henri Nouwen, listen to my friend Sister Marina: It's all in the Bible.

☙

Virtue: Surrender
As Lived and Taught by Jesus: Matthew 26:39
In the most difficult times of life and ministry, we can find comfort in the garden with Jesus, who surrendered all to God, but not without inner struggle.

> He advanced a little and fell prostrate in prayer saying,
> "My Father, if it is possible, let this cup pass from me;
> yet, not as I will, but as you will."

Christ's humanity joins with ours, but we can join in his divine acceptance of what God was calling him to do.

☙

TO PONDER

When have I found it difficult to surrender to God's will in ministry?

How can I find time to listen for his voice?

How often do I turn to the Bible to let God speak to me?

Who is a role model for me in living the faith, in surrendering to God's will?

CONCLUSION

I started this book with St. Paul's advice to the Colossians to put on compassion, kindness, humility, gentleness, and patience. I've only touched on some of those and added a few more items to my friend Paul's list. Most importantly, I am mindful of how he ends that list: "And over all these put on love, that is, the bond of perfection" (3:14).

We are, after all, aiming for perfection, to be holy as God is holy. For most of us, it takes time to come even close to attaining that holiness. We have to remember that this is a lifelong journey of love. Just the other day I was kneeling before the Blessed Sacrament when a song landed in my head: *The Long and Winding Road* by The Beatles. I hadn't heard or thought about that song in years. (God uses all manner of things to speak to us, doesn't he?) Yes, the journey toward holiness is long and winding, but we don't travel it alone. The Word was made flesh and dwells among us, walks that long and winding road along with us. We, too, are called to walk with others in parish life, and to allow them to walk with us just as Jesus walked with sinners, women, the sick, and the possessed.

We are called to stock up on every virtue so that we can bring God's presence to one another along this journey, remembering that Jesus never leaves us. He is with us always, even and most powerfully in the mess of this life — even in the mess of parish life. He is with us until the end of time. He is here to keep our supply closet fully stocked with faith, hope, and a sense of humor as well as humility, fortitude, courage, eutrapelia, gentleness, hospitality, gratitude, prudence, self-worth, surrender, and, as the bond of perfection over all of that, love.

So take yourself to the tabernacle where the presence of Christ resides, offering us every virtue needed, because he embodies all of them.

We should go there often to share in the goodness of the Lord, to give ourselves to him as he gives himself to us. And when you feel you fall short, just keep trying to surrender it all to him: Keep being the person you are called to be, the loving Christian God's grace is empowering you to be. Sure, there is plenty we have to "do," but mostly let's be holy as he is holy, each in our own unique and human way. Let's love each other well. Our families, pastors, and fellow parishioners need us almost as much as we need them. And let's not forget to take time to kneel before the tabernacle and give thanks to the Lord, for he is good. Consider taking this book with you there, sit in his presence, offer a smile, and linger in Love.

Let us pray …

A PRAYER FOR PARISH MINISTERS

God of love and infinite mercy,
I come before you with an open heart, asking you to fill
    me today
with everything I need to be more like you,
to be holy as you are holy.
Fill me with faith, to trust in you;
Fill me with humility, to lead like you;
Fill me with love, to love like you;
Fill me with fortitude and courage, to speak your truth;
Fill me with relaxation, to be at peace;
Fill me with gentleness, to be kind like you;
Fill me with the spirit of hospitality, to be compassionate
    like you;
Fill me with gratitude, to be generous like you;
Fill me with prudence, to be wise like you;
Fill me with laughter, to rejoice with you;
Fill me with self-worth, to be strong like you;
Fill me with hope, to persevere like you;
Fill me with the desire to surrender all to your holy will.
Sustain me in what you have called me to and help me to
    love your people well.
I ask this through Christ, your Son, and our Lord.
Amen.

ACKNOWLEDGMENTS

I am grateful to so many who helped in making this book a reality.

First, I am grateful to family and friends who put up with my discussions on parish ministry and offered valuable insights. I am especially grateful to my sister, who let me use her peaceful getaway for a place to pray and write, and to my brother and sister-in-law for letting me use their beach home and also offering thoughts on this manuscript. Many thanks to Our Sunday Visitor and editor Jaymie Wolfe, who helped make this book 100 percent better. Finally, I give thanks to my pastor and colleagues in parish ministry for letting me share our stories. Above all, I thank God for leading me to this parish community that I love and where I serve, all for the greater glory of God and his kingdom.

ABOUT THE AUTHOR

Karen Baker works full-time in parish ministry, serving as Office Manager at Mary, Queen of Peace Catholic Church in Mandeville, Louisiana. She enjoys designing bulletins, composing creative emails, and handling the surprises that come along every day. She is grateful to work with clergy who follow the model of Jesus, colleagues who labor joyfully in the vineyard, and parishioners who make it all worthwhile.

After thirty years as a journalist in Orlando, Florida, and New Orleans, she received her master's degree in pastoral studies from Loyola University in New Orleans in 2012. She also completed a program in lay ecclesial ministry through Notre Dame Seminary in New Orleans and was commissioned by Archbishop Gregory M. Aymond in January 2015.

Karen lives in Covington, Louisiana, with her family. When not pondering the mysteries of parish life, she enjoys long walks, good books, and spending time with friends.